TOPIC _____   DATE _____

PERSON 1 _____   PERSON 2 _____

Additional Characters

_____
_____
_____

Person 1 Description

How the fight went down

_____
_____
_____
_____
_____

Person 2 Description

Memorable Lines

_____
_____
_____

Outcome

My secret notes

_____
_____
_____

SOMEONE ELSE'S CONFLICT

FIGHT

TOPIC _____ DATE _____

PERSON 1 _____ PERSON 2 _____

Additional Characters

_____
_____
_____

Person 1 Description

How the fight went down

_____
_____
_____
_____
_____

Person 2 Description

Memorable Lines

_____
_____
_____

Outcome

My secret notes

_____
_____
_____

SOMEONE ELSE'S CONFLICT

FIGHT

TOPIC _____   DATE _____

PERSON 1 _____   PERSON 2 _____

Additional Characters

_____
_____
_____

Person 1 Description

How the fight went down

_____
_____
_____
_____
_____

Person 2 Description

Memorable Lines

_____
_____
_____

Outcome

My secret notes

_____
_____
_____

SOMEONE ELSE'S CONFLICT

FIGHT

TOPIC _____   DATE _____

PERSON 1 _____   PERSON 2 _____

Additional Characters

_____
_____
_____

Person 1 Description

How the fight went down

_____
_____
_____
_____
_____

Person 2 Description

Memorable Lines

_____
_____

Outcome

My secret notes

_____
_____
_____

SOMEONE ELSE'S CONFLICT

FIGHT

TOPIC _____ DATE _____

PERSON 1 _____ PERSON 2 _____

Additional Characters

_____
_____
_____

How the fight went down

_____
_____
_____
_____
_____

Memorable Lines

_____
_____
_____

My secret notes

_____
_____
_____

Person 1 Description

_____
_____
_____

Person 2 Description

_____
_____
_____

Outcome

_____
_____
_____

SOMEONE ELSE'S CONFLICT

FIGHT

TOPIC _____   DATE _____

PERSON 1 _____   PERSON 2 _____

Additional Characters

_____
_____
_____

How the fight went down

_____
_____
_____
_____

Memorable Lines

_____
_____
_____

My secret notes

_____
_____
_____

Person 1 Description

Person 2 Description

Outcome

SOMEONE ELSE'S CONFLICT

FIGHT

TOPIC _____   DATE _____

PERSON 1 _____   PERSON 2 _____

Additional Characters
_____
_____
_____

How the fight went down
_____
_____
_____
_____
_____

Memorable Lines
_____
_____

My secret notes
_____
_____
_____

Person 1 Description

Person 2 Description

Outcome

SOMEONE ELSE'S CONFLICT

FIGHT

TOPIC _____   DATE _____

PERSON 1 _____   PERSON 2 _____

Additional Characters

_____
_____
_____

How the fight went down

_____
_____
_____
_____

Memorable Lines

_____
_____
_____

My secret notes

_____
_____
_____

Person 1 Description

Person 2 Description

Outcome

SOMEONE ELSE'S CONFLICT

FIGHT

TCPIC _____ DATE _____

PERSON 1 _____ PERSON 2 _____

Additional Characters
_____
_____
_____

How the fight went down
_____
_____
_____
_____
_____

Memorable Lines
_____
_____
_____

My secret notes
_____
_____
_____

Person 1 Description

Person 2 Description

Outcome

SOMEONE ELSE'S CONFLICT

FIGHT

TOPIC _____   DATE _____

PERSON 1 _____   PERSON 2 _____

Additional Characters

_____
_____
_____

How the fight went down

_____
_____
_____
_____
_____

Memorable Lines

_____
_____
_____

My secret notes

_____
_____
_____

Person 1 Description

Person 2 Description

Outcome

SOMEONE ELSE'S CONFLICT

FIGHT

TOPIC _____   DATE _____

PERSON 1 _____   PERSON 2 _____

Additional Characters
_____
_____
_____

How the fight went down
_____
_____
_____
_____
_____

Memorable Lines
_____
_____

My secret notes
_____
_____
_____

Person 1 Description

Person 2 Description

Outcome

SOMEONE ELSE'S CONFLICT

FIGHT

TOPIC _____   DATE _____

PERSON 1 _____   PERSON 2 _____

Additional Characters
_____
_____
_____

Person 1 Description

How the fight went down
_____
_____
_____
_____
_____

Person 2 Description

Memorable Lines
_____
_____

Outcome

My secret notes
_____
_____
_____

SOMEONE ELSE'S CONFLICT

FIGHT

TOPIC _____   DATE _____

PERSON 1 _____   PERSON 2 _____

Additional Characters
_____
_____
_____

How the fight went down
_____
_____
_____
_____

Memorable Lines
_____
_____

My secret notes
_____
_____

Person 1 Description

Person 2 Description

Outcome

SOMEONE ELSE'S CONFLICT

FIGHT

TOPIC _____   DATE _____

PERSON 1 _____   PERSON 2 _____

Additional Characters
_____
_____
_____

Person 1 Description

How the fight went down
_____
_____
_____
_____
_____

Person 2 Description

Memorable Lines
_____
_____
_____

Outcome

My secret notes
_____
_____
_____

SOMEONE ELSE'S CONFLICT

FIGHT

TCPIC _____ DATE _____

PERSON 1 _____ PERSON 2 _____

Additional Characters

_____
_____
_____

How the fight went down

_____
_____
_____
_____

Memorable Lines

_____
_____
_____

My secret notes

_____
_____
_____

Person 1 Description

Person 2 Description

Outcome

SOMEONE ELSE'S CONFLICT

FIGHT

TOPIC _____   DATE _____

PERSON 1 _____ PERSON 2 _____

Additional Characters

_____
_____
_____

How the fight went down

_____
_____
_____
_____

Memorable Lines

_____
_____
_____

My secret notes

_____
_____
_____

Person 1 Description

Person 2 Description

Outcome

SOMEONE ELSE'S CONFLICT

FIGHT

TOPIC _____ DATE _____

PERSON 1 _____ PERSON 2 _____

Additional Characters

_____
_____
_____

Person 1 Description

How the fight went down

_____
_____
_____
_____
_____

Person 2 Description

Memorable Lines

_____
_____
_____

Outcome

My secret notes

_____
_____

SOMEONE ELSE'S CONFLICT

FIGHT

TOPIC _____   DATE _____

PERSON 1 _____   PERSON 2 _____

Additional Characters

_____
_____
_____

Person 1 Description

How the fight went down

_____
_____
_____
_____

Person 2 Description

Memorable Lines

_____
_____

Outcome

My secret notes

_____
_____

SOMEONE ELSE'S CONFLICT

FIGHT

TOPIC _____   DATE _____

PERSON 1 _____   PERSON 2 _____

Additional Characters

_____
_____

How the fight went down

_____
_____
_____
_____

Memorable Lines

_____
_____

My secret notes

_____
_____

Person 1 Description

Person 2 Description

Outcome

SOMEONE ELSE'S CONFLICT

FIGHT

TOPIC _____   DATE _____

PERSON 1 _____   PERSON 2 _____

Additional Characters
_____
_____

Person 1 Description

How the fight went down
_____
_____
_____
_____

Person 2 Description

Memorable Lines
_____
_____
_____

Outcome

My secret notes
_____
_____
_____

SOMEONE ELSE'S CONFLICT

FIGHT

TOPIC _____ DATE _____

PERSON 1 _____ PERSON 2 _____

Additional Characters

_____
_____
_____

Person 1 Description

_____
_____
_____
_____

How the fight went down

_____
_____
_____
_____
_____

Person 2 Description

_____
_____
_____
_____

Memorable Lines

_____
_____
_____

Outcome

_____
_____

My secret notes

_____
_____

SOMEONE ELSE'S CONFLICT

FIGHT

TOPIC _____   DATE _____

PERSON 1 _____   PERSON 2 _____

Additional Characters
_____
_____
_____

Person 1 Description

How the fight went down
_____
_____
_____
_____

Person 2 Description

Memorable Lines
_____
_____
_____

Outcome

My secret notes
_____
_____
_____

SOMEONE ELSE'S CONFLICT

FIGHT

TOPIC _____   DATE _____

PERSON 1 _____   PERSON 2 _____

Additional Characters

_____
_____

Person 1 Description

How the fight went down

_____
_____
_____
_____

Person 2 Description

Memorable Lines

_____
_____

Outcome

My secret notes

_____
_____

SOMEONE ELSE'S CONFLICT

FIGHT

TOPIC _____ DATE _____

PERSON 1 _____ PERSON 2 _____

Additional Characters
_____
_____
_____

Person 1 Description

How the fight went down
_____
_____
_____
_____

Person 2 Description

Memorable Lines
_____
_____
_____

Outcome

My secret notes
_____
_____
_____

SOMEONE ELSE'S CONFLICT

FIGHT

TOPIC _____ DATE _____

PERSON 1 _____ PERSON 2 _____

Additional Characters

_____
_____
_____

Person 1 Description

How the fight went down

_____
_____
_____
_____
_____

Person 2 Description

Memorable Lines

_____
_____
_____

Outcome

My secret notes

_____
_____
_____

SOMEONE ELSE'S CONFLICT

FIGHT

TOPIC _____ DATE _____

PERSON 1 _____ PERSON 2 _____

Additional Characters

Person 1 Description

How the fight went down

Person 2 Description

Memorable Lines

Outcome

My secret notes

SOMEONE ELSE'S CONFLICT

FIGHT

TOPIC _____   DATE _____

PERSON 1 _____ PERSON 2 _____

Additional Characters
_____
_____
_____

Person 1 Description

How the fight went down
_____
_____
_____
_____

Person 2 Description

Memorable Lines
_____
_____
_____

Outcome

My secret notes
_____
_____

SOMEONE ELSE'S CONFLICT

FIGHT

TOPIC _____ DATE _____

PERSON 1 _____ PERSON 2 _____

Additional Characters
_____
_____
_____

Person 1 Description

How the fight went down
_____
_____
_____
_____

Person 2 Description

Memorable Lines
_____
_____
_____

Outcome

My secret notes
_____
_____
_____

SOMEONE ELSE'S CONFLICT

FIGHT

TOPIC _____   DATE _____

PERSON 1 _____   PERSON 2 _____

Additional Characters

_____
_____
_____

Person 1 Description

How the fight went down

_____
_____
_____
_____

Person 2 Description

Memorable Lines

_____
_____
_____

Outcome

My secret notes

_____
_____
_____

SOMEONE ELSE'S CONFLICT

FIGHT

TOPIC _____   DATE _____

PERSON 1 _____   PERSON 2 _____

Additional Characters

Person 1 Description

How the fight went down

Person 2 Description

Memorable Lines

Outcome

My secret notes

SOMEONE ELSE'S CONFLICT

FIGHT

TOPIC _____   DATE _____

PERSON 1 _____   PERSON 2 _____

Additional Characters

_____
_____
_____

Person 1 Description

How the fight went down

_____
_____
_____
_____

Person 2 Description

Memorable Lines

_____
_____

Outcome

My secret notes

_____
_____
_____

SOMEONE ELSE'S CONFLICT

FIGHT

TOPIC _____   DATE _____

PERSON 1 _____   PERSON 2 _____

Additional Characters

_____
_____
_____

Person 1 Description

How the fight went down

_____
_____
_____
_____

Person 2 Description

Memorable Lines

_____
_____
_____

Outcome

My secret notes

_____
_____
_____

SOMEONE ELSE'S CONFLICT

FIGHT

TOPIC _____ DATE _____

PERSON 1 _____ PERSON 2 _____

Additional Characters

_____
_____
_____

Person 1 Description

How the fight went down

_____
_____
_____
_____

Person 2 Description

Memorable Lines

_____
_____
_____

Outcome

My secret notes

_____
_____

SOMEONE ELSE'S CONFLICT

FIGHT

TOPIC _____   DATE _____

PERSON 1 _____   PERSON 2 _____

Additional Characters

_____
_____
_____

Person 1 Description

How the fight went down

_____
_____
_____

Person 2 Description

Memorable Lines

_____
_____
_____

Outcome

My secret notes

_____
_____
_____

SOMEONE ELSE'S CONFLICT

FIGHT

TOPIC _____ DATE _____

PERSON 1 _____ PERSON 2 _____

Additional Characters

_____
_____
_____

Person 1 Description

How the fight went down

_____
_____
_____
_____
_____

Person 2 Description

Memorable Lines

_____
_____
_____

Outcome

My secret notes

_____
_____
_____

SOMEONE ELSE'S CONFLICT

FIGHT

TOPIC _____   DATE _____

PERSON 1 _____   PERSON 2 _____

Additional Characters

_____
_____
_____

How the fight went down

_____
_____
_____
_____
_____

Memorable Lines

_____
_____
_____

My secret notes

_____
_____
_____

Person 1 Description

Person 2 Description

Outcome

SOMEONE ELSE'S CONFLICT

FIGHT

TOPIC _____ DATE _____

PERSON 1 _____ PERSON 2 _____

Additional Characters

Person 1 Description

How the fight went down

Person 2 Description

Memorable Lines

Outcome

My secret notes

SOMEONE ELSE'S CONFLICT

FIGHT

TOPIC _____ DATE _____

PERSON 1 _____ PERSON 2 _____

Additional Characters

_____
_____
_____

Person 1 Description

How the fight went down

_____
_____
_____
_____

Person 2 Description

Memorable Lines

_____
_____
_____

Outcome

My secret notes

_____
_____
_____

SOMEONE ELSE'S CONFLICT

FIGHT

TOPIC _____   DATE _____

PERSON 1 _____   PERSON 2 _____

Additional Characters

_____
_____

Person 1 Description

_____

How the fight went down

_____
_____
_____

Person 2 Description

_____

Memorable Lines

_____
_____

Outcome

_____

My secret notes

_____
_____

SOMEONE ELSE'S CONFLICT

FIGHT

TOPIC _____   DATE _____

PERSON 1 _____ PERSON 2 _____

Additional Characters

_____
_____
_____

Person 1 Description

_____
_____
_____

How the fight went down

_____
_____
_____
_____
_____

Person 2 Description

_____
_____
_____

Memorable Lines

_____
_____
_____

Outcome

_____
_____

My secret notes

_____
_____
_____

SOMEONE ELSE'S CONFLICT

FIGHT

TOPIC _____   DATE _____

PERSON 1 _____   PERSON 2 _____

Additional Characters

_____
_____
_____

How the fight went down

_____
_____
_____
_____

Memorable Lines

_____
_____
_____

My secret notes

_____
_____
_____

Person 1 Description

Person 2 Description

Outcome

SOMEONE ELSE'S CONFLICT

FIGHT

TOPIC _____ DATE _____

PERSON 1 _____ PERSON 2 _____

Additional Characters

_____
_____

Person 1 Description

How the fight went down

_____
_____
_____
_____

Person 2 Description

Memorable Lines

_____
_____
_____

Outcome

My secret notes

_____
_____
_____

SOMEONE ELSE'S CONFLICT

FIGHT

TOPIC _____   DATE _____

PERSON 1 _____   PERSON 2 _____

Additional Characters

_____
_____
_____

How the fight went down

_____
_____
_____
_____

Memorable Lines

_____
_____

My secret notes

_____
_____
_____

Person 1 Description

Person 2 Description

Outcome

SOMEONE ELSE'S CONFLICT

FIGHT

TOPIC _____   DATE _____

PERSON 1 _____   PERSON 2 _____

Additional Characters

_____
_____
_____

Person 1 Description

How the fight went down

_____
_____
_____
_____
_____

Person 2 Description

Memorable Lines

_____
_____
_____

Outcome

My secret notes

_____
_____
_____

SOMEONE ELSE'S CONFLICT

FIGHT

TOPIC _____ DATE _____

PERSON 1 _____ PERSON 2 _____

Additional Characters

_____
_____
_____

Person 1 Description

How the fight went down

_____
_____
_____
_____

Person 2 Description

Memorable Lines

_____
_____
_____

Outcome

My secret notes

_____
_____
_____

SOMEONE ELSE'S CONFLICT

FIGHT

TOPIC _____ DATE _____

PERSON 1 _____ PERSON 2 _____

Additional Characters

_____
_____

How the fight went down

_____
_____
_____
_____

Memorable Lines

_____
_____

My secret notes

_____
_____

Person 1 Description

Person 2 Description

Outcome

SOMEONE ELSE'S CONFLICT

FIGHT

TCPIC _____   DATE _____

PERSON 1 _____   PERSON 2 _____

Additional Characters

_____
_____
_____

How the fight went down

_____
_____
_____
_____

Memorable Lines

_____
_____

My secret notes

_____
_____
_____

Person 1 Description

Person 2 Description

Outcome

SOMEONE ELSE'S CONFLICT

FIGHT

TOPIC _____ DATE _____

PERSON 1 _____ PERSON 2 _____

Additional Characters
_____
_____
_____

Person 1 Description

How the fight went down
_____
_____
_____
_____

Person 2 Description

Memorable Lines
_____
_____
_____

Outcome

My secret notes
_____
_____
_____

SOMEONE ELSE'S CONFLICT

FIGHT

TOPIC _____   DATE _____

PERSON 1 _____   PERSON 2 _____

Additional Characters

_____
_____
_____

Person 1 Description

_____
_____
_____
_____

How the fight went down

_____
_____
_____
_____

Person 2 Description

_____
_____
_____
_____

Memorable Lines

_____
_____

Outcome

_____
_____

My secret notes

_____
_____

SOMEONE ELSE'S CONFLICT

FIGHT

TOPIC _____   DATE _____

PERSON 1 _____   PERSON 2 _____

Additional Characters

_____
_____
_____

Person 1 Description

How the fight went down

_____
_____
_____
_____

Person 2 Description

Memorable Lines

_____
_____
_____

Outcome

My secret notes

_____
_____
_____

SOMEONE ELSE'S CONFLICT

FIGHT

TOPIC _____ DATE _____

PERSON 1 _____ PERSON 2 _____

Additional Characters

_____
_____
_____

How the fight went down

_____
_____
_____
_____

Memorable Lines

_____
_____

My secret notes

_____
_____

Person 1 Description

Person 2 Description

Outcome

SOMEONE ELSE'S CONFLICT

FIGHT

TOPIC _____ DATE _____

PERSON 1 _____ PERSON 2 _____

Additional Characters

_____
_____
_____

Person 1 Description

How the fight went down

_____
_____
_____
_____

Person 2 Description

Memorable Lines

_____
_____
_____

Outcome

My secret notes

_____
_____
_____

SOMEONE ELSE'S CONFLICT

FIGHT

TOPIC _____   DATE _____

PERSON 1 _____   PERSON 2 _____

Additional Characters

_____
_____
_____

How the fight went down

_____
_____
_____
_____

Memorable Lines

_____
_____

My secret notes

_____
_____

Person 1 Description

Person 2 Description

Outcome

SOMEONE ELSE'S CONFLICT

FIGHT

TOPIC _____   DATE _____

PERSON 1 _____   PERSON 2 _____

Additional Characters

_____
_____
_____

How the fight went down

_____
_____
_____
_____

Memorable Lines

_____
_____

My secret notes

_____
_____
_____

Person 1 Description

Person 2 Description

Outcome

SOMEONE ELSE'S CONFLICT

FIGHT

TOPIC _____ DATE _____

PERSON 1 _____ PERSON 2 _____

Additional Characters

_____
_____
_____

How the fight went down

_____
_____
_____
_____

Memorable Lines

_____
_____

My secret notes

_____
_____

Person 1 Description

Person 2 Description

Outcome

SOMEONE ELSE'S CONFLICT

FIGHT

TOPIC _____   DATE _____

PERSON 1 _____ PERSON 2 _____

Additional Characters

_____
_____
_____

How the fight went down

_____
_____
_____
_____
_____

Memorable Lines

_____
_____
_____

My secret notes

_____
_____
_____

Person 1 Description

Person 2 Description

Outcome

SOMEONE ELSE'S CONFLICT

FIGHT

TOPIC _____ DATE _____

PERSON 1 _____ PERSON 2 _____

Additional Characters

_____
_____
_____

How the fight went down

_____
_____
_____
_____

Memorable Lines

_____
_____

My secret notes

_____
_____

Person 1 Description

Person 2 Description

Outcome

SOMEONE ELSE'S CONFLICT

FIGHT

TOPIC _____   DATE _____

PERSON 1 _____   PERSON 2 _____

Additional Characters

_____
_____
_____

Person 1 Description

How the fight went down

_____
_____
_____
_____
_____

Person 2 Description

Memorable Lines

_____
_____
_____

Outcome

My secret notes

_____
_____
_____

SOMEONE ELSE'S CONFLICT

FIGHT

TOPIC _____   DATE _____

PERSON 1 _____   PERSON 2 _____

Additional Characters

_____
_____
_____

How the fight went down

_____
_____
_____
_____

Memorable Lines

_____
_____

My secret notes

_____
_____
_____

Person 1 Description

Person 2 Description

Outcome

SOMEONE ELSE'S CONFLICT

FIGHT

TOPIC _____ DATE _____

PERSON 1 _____ PERSON 2 _____

Additional Characters

_____
_____
_____

Person 1 Description

How the fight went down

_____
_____
_____
_____

Person 2 Description

Memorable Lines

_____
_____
_____

Outcome

My secret notes

_____
_____
_____

SOMEONE ELSE'S CONFLICT

FIGHT

TOPIC _____ DATE _____

PERSON 1 _____ PERSON 2 _____

Additional Characters

_____
_____
_____

Person 1 Description

How the fight went down

_____
_____
_____

Person 2 Description

Memorable Lines

_____
_____

Outcome

My secret notes

_____
_____

SOMEONE ELSE'S CONFLICT

FIGHT

TOPIC _____   DATE _____

PERSON 1 _____   PERSON 2 _____

Additional Characters

_____
_____
_____

How the fight went down

_____
_____
_____
_____

Memorable Lines

_____
_____
_____

My secret notes

_____
_____
_____

Person 1 Description

Person 2 Description

Outcome

SOMEONE ELSE'S CONFLICT

FIGHT

TOPIC _____ DATE _____

PERSON 1 _____ PERSON 2 _____

Additional Characters

_____
_____
_____

How the fight went down

_____
_____
_____
_____

Memorable Lines

_____
_____
_____

My secret notes

_____
_____
_____

Person 1 Description

Person 2 Description

Outcome

SOMEONE ELSE'S CONFLICT

FIGHT

TOPIC _____   DATE _____

PERSON 1 _____ PERSON 2 _____

Additional Characters

_____
_____
_____

Person 1 Description

How the fight went down

_____
_____
_____
_____

Person 2 Description

Memorable Lines

_____
_____

Outcome

My secret notes

_____
_____

SOMEONE ELSE'S CONFLICT

FIGHT

TOPIC _____ DATE _____

PERSON 1 _____ PERSON 2 _____

Additional Characters

_____
_____
_____

Person 1 Description

_____
_____
_____

How the fight went down

_____
_____
_____
_____

Person 2 Description

_____
_____
_____

Memorable Lines

_____
_____

Outcome

_____
_____

My secret notes

_____
_____

SOMEONE ELSE'S CONFLICT

FIGHT

TOPIC _____   DATE _____

PERSON 1 _____   PERSON 2 _____

Additional Characters

_____
_____
_____

Person 1 Description

How the fight went down

_____
_____
_____
_____

Person 2 Description

Memorable Lines

_____
_____

Outcome

My secret notes

_____
_____
_____

SOMEONE ELSE'S CONFLICT

FIGHT

TOPIC _____ DATE _____

PERSON 1 _____ PERSON 2 _____

Additional Characters

_____
_____
_____

How the fight went down

_____
_____
_____
_____

Memorable Lines

_____
_____

My secret notes

_____
_____

Person 1 Description

Person 2 Description

Outcome

SOMEONE ELSE'S CONFLICT

FIGHT

TOPIC _____   DATE _____

PERSON 1 _____   PERSON 2 _____

Additional Characters

_____
_____
_____

How the fight went down

_____
_____
_____
_____

Memorable Lines

_____
_____
_____

My secret notes

_____
_____
_____

Person 1 Description

Person 2 Description

Outcome

SOMEONE ELSE'S CONFLICT

FIGHT

TOPIC _____ DATE _____

PERSON 1 _____ PERSON 2 _____

Additional Characters

_____
_____
_____

How the fight went down

_____
_____
_____
_____

Memorable Lines

_____
_____

My secret notes

_____
_____

Person 1 Description

Person 2 Description

Outcome

SOMEONE ELSE'S CONFLICT

FIGHT

TOPIC _____ DATE _____

PERSON 1 _____ PERSON 2 _____

Additional Characters

_____
_____
_____

How the fight went down

_____
_____
_____
_____

Memorable Lines

_____
_____
_____

My secret notes

_____
_____
_____

Person 1 Description

Person 2 Description

Outcome

SOMEONE ELSE'S CONFLICT

FIGHT

TCPIC _____   DATE _____

PERSON 1 _____   PERSON 2 _____

Additional Characters

_____
_____
_____

How the fight went down

_____
_____
_____
_____

Memorable Lines

_____
_____

My secret notes

_____
_____

Person 1 Description

_____
_____
_____
_____

Person 2 Description

_____
_____
_____
_____

Outcome

_____
_____
_____

SOMEONE ELSE'S CONFLICT

FIGHT

TOPIC _____ DATE _____

PERSON 1 _____ PERSON 2 _____

Additional Characters
_____
_____
_____

How the fight went down
_____
_____
_____
_____
_____

Memorable Lines
_____
_____
_____

My secret notes
_____
_____
_____

Person 1 Description

Person 2 Description

Outcome

SOMEONE ELSE'S CONFLICT

FIGHT

TOPIC _____   DATE _____

PERSON 1 _____   PERSON 2 _____

Additional Characters

_____
_____
_____

How the fight went down

_____
_____
_____
_____

Memorable Lines

_____
_____
_____

My secret notes

_____
_____

Person 1 Description

_____
_____
_____
_____

Person 2 Description

_____
_____
_____
_____

Outcome

_____
_____
_____
_____

SOMEONE ELSE'S CONFLICT

FIGHT

TOPIC _____ DATE _____

PERSON 1 _____ PERSON 2 _____

Additional Characters

_____

_____

_____

Person 1 Description

How the fight went down

_____

_____

_____

_____

Person 2 Description

Memorable Lines

_____

_____

Outcome

My secret notes

_____

_____

SOMEONE ELSE'S CONFLICT

FIGHT

TOPIC _____   DATE _____

PERSON 1 _____   PERSON 2 _____

Additional Characters

_____
_____
_____

Person 1 Description

How the fight went down

_____
_____
_____
_____

Person 2 Description

Memorable Lines

_____
_____

Outcome

My secret notes

_____
_____

SOMEONE ELSE'S CONFLICT

FIGHT

TOPIC _____ DATE _____

PERSON 1 _____ PERSON 2 _____

Additional Characters

_____
_____
_____

How the fight went down

_____
_____
_____
_____

Memorable Lines

_____
_____

My secret notes

_____
_____

Person 1 Description

Person 2 Description

Outcome

SOMEONE ELSE'S CONFLICT

FIGHT

TOPIC _____ DATE _____

PERSON 1 _____ PERSON 2 _____

Additional Characters

_____
_____
_____

How the fight went down

_____
_____
_____
_____

Memorable Lines

_____
_____

My secret notes

_____
_____

Person 1 Description

Person 2 Description

Outcome

SOMEONE ELSE'S CONFLICT

FIGHT

TOPIC _____   DATE _____

PERSON 1 _____   PERSON 2 _____

Additional Characters

_____
_____
_____

Person 1 Description

How the fight went down

_____
_____
_____
_____

Person 2 Description

Memorable Lines

_____
_____
_____

Outcome

My secret notes

_____
_____
_____

SOMEONE ELSE'S CONFLICT

FIGHT

TOPIC _____   DATE _____

PERSON 1 _____   PERSON 2 _____

Additional Characters

_____
_____
_____

Person 1 Description

How the fight went down

_____
_____
_____

Person 2 Description

Memorable Lines

_____
_____
_____

Outcome

My secret notes

_____
_____
_____

SOMEONE ELSE'S CONFLICT

FIGHT

TOPIC _____   DATE _____

PERSON 1 _____   PERSON 2 _____

Additional Characters

_____
_____
_____

How the fight went down

_____
_____
_____
_____

Memorable Lines

_____
_____
_____

My secret notes

_____
_____
_____

Person 1 Description

Person 2 Description

Outcome

SOMEONE ELSE'S CONFLICT

FIGHT

TOPIC _____   DATE _____

PERSON 1 _____ PERSON 2 _____

Additional Characters

_____
_____
_____

How the fight went down

_____
_____
_____
_____

Memorable Lines

_____
_____

My secret notes

_____
_____

Person 1 Description

Person 2 Description

Outcome

SOMEONE ELSE'S CONFLICT

FIGHT

TOPIC _____ DATE _____

PERSON 1 _____ PERSON 2 _____

Additional Characters
_____
_____
_____

Person 1 Description

How the fight went down
_____
_____
_____
_____

Person 2 Description

Memorable Lines
_____
_____
_____

Outcome

My secret notes
_____
_____
_____

SOMEONE ELSE'S CONFLICT

FIGHT

TOPIC _____   DATE _____

PERSON 1 _____   PERSON 2 _____

Additional Characters
_____
_____
_____

How the fight went down
_____
_____
_____
_____
_____

Memorable Lines
_____
_____
_____

My secret notes
_____
_____
_____

Person 1 Description

Person 2 Description

Outcome

SOMEONE ELSE'S CONFLICT

FIGHT

TOPIC _____ DATE _____

PERSON 1 _____ PERSON 2 _____

Additional Characters

_____
_____
_____

Person 1 Description

How the fight went down

_____
_____
_____
_____

Person 2 Description

Memorable Lines

_____
_____
_____

Outcome

My secret notes

_____
_____
_____

SOMEONE ELSE'S CONFLICT

FIGHT

TOPIC _____   DATE _____

PERSON 1 _____ PERSON 2 _____

Additional Characters
_____
_____
_____

Person 1 Description

How the fight went down
_____
_____
_____
_____

Person 2 Description

Memorable Lines
_____
_____

Outcome

My secret notes
_____
_____

SOMEONE ELSE'S CONFLICT

FIGHT

TOPIC _____   DATE _____

PERSON 1 _____ PERSON 2 _____

Additional Characters
_____
_____
_____

Person 1 Description

How the fight went down
_____
_____
_____
_____
_____

Person 2 Description

Memorable Lines
_____
_____
_____

Outcome

My secret notes
_____
_____
_____

SOMEONE ELSE'S CONFLICT

FIGHT

TOPIC _____   DATE _____

PERSON 1 _____   PERSON 2 _____

Additional Characters

_____
_____
_____

Person 1 Description

_____
_____
_____

How the fight went down

_____
_____
_____
_____

Person 2 Description

_____
_____
_____

Memorable Lines

_____
_____
_____

Outcome

_____
_____

My secret notes

_____
_____
_____

SOMEONE ELSE'S CONFLICT

FIGHT

TOPIC _____   DATE _____

PERSON 1 _____   PERSON 2 _____

Additional Characters

_____
_____
_____

How the fight went down

_____
_____
_____
_____

Memorable Lines

_____
_____

My secret notes

_____
_____

Person 1 Description

Person 2 Description

Outcome

SOMEONE ELSE'S CONFLICT

FIGHT

TOPIC _____ DATE _____

PERSON 1 _____ PERSON 2 _____

Additional Characters

_____
_____
_____

How the fight went down

_____
_____
_____
_____
_____

Memorable Lines

_____
_____

My secret notes

_____
_____
_____

Person 1 Description

Person 2 Description

Outcome

SOMEONE ELSE'S CONFLICT

FIGHT

TOPIC _____   DATE _____

PERSON 1 _____   PERSON 2 _____

Additional Characters

_____
_____
_____

How the fight went down

_____
_____
_____
_____

Memorable Lines

_____
_____

My secret notes

_____
_____

Person 1 Description

Person 2 Description

Outcome

SOMEONE ELSE'S CONFLICT

FIGHT

TOPIC _____   DATE _____

PERSON 1 _____   PERSON 2 _____

Additional Characters

_____
_____
_____

How the fight went down

_____
_____
_____
_____

Memorable Lines

_____
_____

My secret notes

_____
_____

Person 1 Description

Person 2 Description

Outcome

SOMEONE ELSE'S CONFLICT

FIGHT

TOPIC _____ DATE _____

PERSON 1 _____ PERSON 2 _____

Additional Characters
_____
_____
_____

Person 1 Description

How the fight went down
_____
_____
_____
_____

Person 2 Description

Memorable Lines
_____
_____
_____

Outcome

My secret notes
_____
_____
_____

SOMEONE ELSE'S CONFLICT

FIGHT

TOPIC _____ DATE _____

PERSON 1 _____ PERSON 2 _____

Additional Characters

_____
_____
_____

How the fight went down

_____
_____
_____
_____

Memorable Lines

_____
_____

My secret notes

_____
_____
_____

Person 1 Description

Person 2 Description

Outcome

SOMEONE ELSE'S CONFLICT

FIGHT

TOPIC _____ DATE _____

PERSON 1 _____ PERSON 2 _____

Additional Characters

_____
_____
_____

Person 1 Description

How the fight went down

_____
_____
_____
_____

Person 2 Description

Memorable Lines

_____
_____

Outcome

My secret notes

_____
_____

SOMEONE ELSE'S CONFLICT

FIGHT

TOPIC _____ DATE _____

PERSON 1 _____ PERSON 2 _____

Additional Characters

_____
_____
_____

How the fight went down

_____
_____
_____
_____

Memorable Lines

_____
_____

My secret notes

_____
_____
_____

Person 1 Description

Person 2 Description

Outcome

SOMEONE ELSE'S CONFLICT

FIGHT

TOPIC _____   DATE _____

PERSON 1 _____   PERSON 2 _____

Additional Characters
_____
_____
_____

Person 1 Description

How the fight went down
_____
_____
_____

Person 2 Description

Memorable Lines
_____
_____
_____

Outcome

My secret notes
_____
_____
_____

SOMEONE ELSE'S CONFLICT

Made in the USA
San Bernardino, CA
02 July 2019